Holding the Dark

Holding the Dark

Melanie Cameron

The Muses' Company Series Editor: Catherine Hunter
Cover design by Terry Gallager/Doowah Design Inc.
Cover photo by Marijke Friesen
Author photo by Curtis Kaltenbaugh

Published with the financial assistance of The Canada Council for the Arts and the Manitoba Arts Council.

Printed and bound in Canada

Canadian Cataloguing in Publication Data

Cameron, Melanie
    Holding the dark

Poems.
ISBN 1-896239-47-1

    I. Title.

PS8555.A51955H64 1999   C811'.54   C99-901089-1
PR9199.3.C2795H64 1999

Contents

Between Dream and Open Eyelid

It happened like this / 9
We are used to looking / 11
She you he I it they we are / 12
It doesn't matter that the grass grows / 14
The sun soaks / 15
Bow to the dark / 16
I didn't know it would go like this / 17
I sit across from a man / 18
The darkness is/the inside/of a woman's body / 19
If I can be in her body / 20
I dreamt two small heads / 21
This man who tells me about the stars / 22
Woman, whose eyes do / 23
There is nothing/to fear / 24
The darkness is a handshake / 25
And the darkness is a room / 26
Looking up through the branches of a tree / 27

A Spoonful of Rain

Stars are hiding / 31
The girl is walking / 33
In the forest, the girl can't help but remember / 34
This prairie fits the girl / 36
The girl watches a sparrow / 37
The girl is trying to think of a language / 38
The girl's mouth is a/magnet… / 39
And the girl's mouth must move / 40
The girl holds wonder / 41
They say Ophelia sang / 42
Imagine/Ophelia, floating / 43

Purple Flowers

Let me tell you how you were / 47
Warm summer nights, I will miss / 48
When he goes to Thailand / 49
These are the things my mouth does in/the dark / 50
You could love me from a distance, as you love / 51
He plugs the ears / 53
Beyond wishing, she wishes / 54
To come back from an afternoon / 55
What a/surprise to find / 56
I love you/furiously / 57
I would walk with you / 58

The Daughters of Silence

Let me/disturb you / 61
This is the one who strangled / 63
A woman crying and crying, a voice echoing / 64
Mom, the tiny blue flowers I picked / 65
What can be so heavy inside / 66
And the mountains are dead, but still / 67
She is screaming / 68
Let's be honest about the dark, let's not / 69
How does it go/in those hot, hot countries... / 71
I once rocked children / 72
The little soldier carries a gun / 73
Little girl with rubber boots / 74
Spanish, so fluid / 75
In my dreams, when they speak Spanish / 76
Juan Manuel, I come back from your country / 78
Convince me / 81

An Open Hand

I am certain women went to the lake / 85
Sitting on this bank / 87
Leaving everything to hang open / 88
A woman carries me / 89
She learned to surrender to the water / 90
You are dark/and your dark hair falls / 91
The sunset is/a woman, dressed / 93
I don't ask/that you break the sky open... / 94
When she opens her hands and holds / 95
She is filled with everything / 97

Floating Ophelia

Ophelia, there was a time when I looked / 101
These flowers float, a final / 102
You say you've never seen anger / 103
Like a mermaid, they say / 104
Everyone thinks Ophelia's dead / 105
So forget the woman who stood at the edge / 106
Ophelia is getting up, leaving / 107
It's like that river flowing past / 108

Acknowledgements / 111

Between Dream and Open Eyelid

$\mathcal{I}$t happened like this.

Darkness claimed her
eyes,
     those months when she had bandages
like a tight fist
        jammed
into each eyesocket.
         The dark
kept pieces of her
         eyes, and left
itself behind, little drops of darkness,
           scattered
across her retinas
     like black stars.

            This explains why
     she never stops touching him with her eyes
closed, why she walks around her rooms alone with her eyes
closed, why she wishes she could write it down with her eyes
closed, why she knows there's darkness
inside her.

Wherever it goes, the darkness takes her
dark eyes with it,
she moves inside it

to Asia when the sun's above her roof,
    to the bottom of the sea,
    swims through hidden caves,
       she rides under the feathers
       of a drifting raven, slips
         along the sidewalk in shadows,
           sneaks through your pupils
           and into your skull,
              dives into an inkwell and comes back up,
              darkness dripping from her body
              in black script.

You can go so many places, come back
with so many things, if
you keep your closed eyes open in the dark,
twin moons in the sky of your head.

We are used to looking
out, locating ourselves against
the wall across the room or
the willow across the field, reaching
its arms into the air and
down again, toward earth. We believe that
the wall and the willow
are real, understandable
in all their parts, though we can't see
inside them, that the earth is real, though
we can't see
her body beyond the horizon,
how it curves. That the sky
is real, though our gaze
can't fall hard
against it, but pierces
light and dark, or maybe the sky
is illusion, though it's the only thing you can trust
to lay its body over you
all day and all night.

Losing your eyes, you lose
day and night, you lose
your understanding of wall and willow
across the way, but you find
the earth under
your feet, completely
understandable, you find
the sky you thought you looked up toward
doesn't know
boundaries
of skin, you find the sky
you thought was out there, is
also around
and inside
you. And the wall. And the willow.

*S*he you he I it they we are
the same thing, words
you shift against each other
as the earth shifts along a fault-line, one
body divided in two, two
bodies moving, we are
moving against ourselves when we move
against each other. I

divide you like a macadamia shell,
fracture your bones trying to get what's inside, I

divide you like a galaxy into constellations,
wanting to see the pictures you make, I

divide you like so many personalities and
all of them, none of them, are
mine. I

divide you like something I could name,
like the mountains and rivers in Jasper, Banff,

I can name every part of you,
point you out to yourself on the map, as though

the water didn't flow into itself,
didn't flow out of clouds, freeze, melt,
and flow
down sides
of mountains, as though the mountains didn't flow
into each other, didn't lie
like the bodies of women and men, tangled
together, everywhere,
a knee
is someone's elbow, a hipbone is a chin, as though
you could divide the mountains as we divide

people,
as we divide the days
of the week, we struggle

to know
exactly where everything starts
and ends.

It doesn't matter that the grass grows
       entangled and
       thick as hair on the body
          of some resting animal,
       wild as an old-growth forest,
          everything in outrageous balance,
       confused as nerves along the edge of a wound,
          firing into the air,

   that I can't touch
       each hair each tree each nerve, the body
       of each animal, forest, wound,

       each blade of grass, growing.

What matters is
       the grass,
       is us, growing
       entangled as
       we touch in the dark.

The sun soaks
into you, the sun sucks
you out of yourself, pulls
deeper shades of you to the surface, unglues
your muscles, joints, teases
liquid from your pores
the way grief draws tears,
                    violence forces blood,
                        and desire, wet.
The sun offers
no choices.

                    But bathing your skin in the moon,
                            you lie so still, you
                    remember warmth, you know
                            what light feels like.
                        You can't ignore
                    the breeze playing through cool leaves,
                    the crickets rubbing their legs together,
                the lilac and primrose opening around you.
                    The moon is not forceful, not
                        easy, in the moonlight you
                    slowly draw yourself out, slowly
                            unfold, sense
                by sense, sound by touch by smell by taste.
                    You learn to bathe yourself in the dark
                and in everything the darkness holds inside.

*B*ow to the dark

if you're willing
to sit in stillness
through this ceremony,

    like the moon,
a great glowing head, always
bowed at night, watching, holding
what she sees, holding us,
in her mind, I see her
face from different angles as she turns
her black night-body,

    like purple flowers,
their petals, veils, wrapped
around faces so intent
on praising the dark
earth they weave their roots through,
they need only
one unshifting eye,

    like the river,
tumbling over itself, falling
prostrate on low land, kissing dark
beds and banks, unceasing,

    like me
above you, then you above me, worshipping
the dark that separates us, by fighting
it, squeezing
our skins together, determined
to press the darkness
out from between us.

$\mathcal{I}$ didn't know it would go like this, I didn't know
I would find you in the dark.

    When I lie
           against you
                 with my eyes
                           closed,
               I bring your body
          with me,
into the darkness,
             I bring your whole
                    body inside
                             me. And in that
              darkness I know you
so much better than hands
               and mouth
                        can know, I know
            you, as though you were
the darkness inside me.

$\mathcal{I}$ sit across from a man
who tells me we all came
from the stars. And the light
against his teeth as he kneads his lip,
and the heat
in his hands when he touches my palm,
and the refraction
of ourselves as we pass through
each other is so bright, hot,
echoed,
has fallen
from somewhere so far away,
and smoulders, burns itself
out, here in this room,
a slow, torturous, beautiful
dying, that you know,
I think I believe him.

The energy of a dying
star, just a few sparks, some dust,
floating.

The darkness is
the inside
of a woman's body.
See what you can't
see, her womb
as a ball of glass, cold
at her centre, like January swallowed
by July.

    One steamy word, a name
          damp against the roof of her mouth, a fragment
            of a dream that stayed
            warm in her gut, never found
            its way to her head at night, tongues
              of breeze licking
              her ankles, sucked
              inside as she uncrosses, recrosses
              her thighs, the moisture
                a man releases into the dark.

                I might have been floating
in that ball of glass, lingering
inside her for a long long time,
and on the coldest day of January, I began
to appear
on the walls of her,
like fingerprints of frost.

If I can be in her body.
If I can grow in her,
a whole skin out of darkness,
something you can touch and taste, just think
what floats in you,
but never develops
bones.

If you watch a man
suck the skin
of a waterdrum, blow
air from his lungs through its pores, creating
the precise balance, the possibility
for perfect resonance,
you will understand

how things suck at you,
blow through you, and stay
balanced.

You will understand that knowing
the darkness is feeling a resonance
emerge from the balance,
just on the other side
of surfaces you strike,
your own skin. Knowing
the darkness is entering
that place everyone sings out to.

$\mathcal{I}$ dreamt two small heads
and thick black hair
with waves like the curl
of ribbon teased against a scissor blade.
We passed them around the circle
face down, and feeling the faces,
we had to guess which one was you.

I didn't need my eyes,
just my fingers to follow
the line of your jaw, your nose, the shape
of your mind, the weight
of you in my palms,
and that hair soaked
with darkness.

I just needed the darkness
and every time the heads came around
the circle, I knew
which one was you.

This man who tells me about the stars
tells me other stories, sometimes
with his eyes his brow his cheeks, sometimes
with his breath his lips his tongue.

One day he tells me I will never lose
my sight because I see everything
in my dreams. And again,
I think I believe him.

Why not believe
when, since
sitting with him in the dark,
I have started to dream
something beyond this place in the immediate
image of his face.

*W*oman, whose eyes do
not see, are you
afraid of the darkness, of falling
with nowhere
to land? Are you
afraid of the way
the darkness holds you,

not

    bobbing in a lattice of boughs and twigs, rubbing
    gently against the skin of an October sky, not
       cocooned in a web in a boarded-up attic where
        no one can find you, the spider's dead, not
           relaxed in a fisherman's net, a steady swinging
           hammock, sunk into the cool belly of the sea,

but

    in the spaces
        between wood
               silk
               rope. Are you

afraid of the way
you hold the dark
    in the spaces between
          marrow and bone
             blood and vein
                dream and open eyelid. Are you

afraid of the way
you fell
from an opening
in black air, cast yourself
here for a while, and

it's only for a while, it's only for
now.

There is nothing
to fear. You are

growing from this dark
ground, lithe poplar, swaying in wind. You are
dropping your leaves, rotting
back into dark
earth, nourishing
yourself. You are

swaying in the wind
on the edge of this bank
and even when the night comes

my arms are tangled
in, I've got my thousand arms tangled in
to you, like branches coming alive in Spring.

The darkness is a handshake.
Some kind of agreement
between
nothing and nothing.

The darkness is that space between
two open palms, that space inside
a fist, it is the skin
around skin.

I could agree
to reach out my hand
to the darkness
of your skin, clasp
the darkness between us, give it
a place to rest for a moment

or keep it, contained
in a deal
to see
everything by daylight.

Or I could reach out my hand
in the dark, make a bet,
give my eyes away, see
nothing, if that would make everything
whole as a foggy night.

I could be shaking hands with some
thing that has
a mind and a body made of darkness.

And the darkness is a room.
Feel how we lie together there,
feel how the walls push out forever,
there are words painted
on the walls, but we don't have to see them
to know what they say. Everything speaks
for itself, in the dark.

Remember how you once told me,
as we lay together in darkness,
that I was in a forest
in your head in the room, I was
lying on the ground
making love to the earth.

How am I doing that? I asked.
You are kissing it, tasting it, moving
against it, writhing, you are
loving yourself.

And there I was,
in that forest in your head in the room
in the dark,
and I was writhing, loving
all of it at once.

Looking up through the branches of a tree,
too many layers to count, and the blue sky beyond,
whose layers I can't begin to make sense of.

Just give me one long, wide strip of grass
laid flat, just give me that one layer
and I will dance
across it, I will dance.

A Spoonful of Rain

Stars are hiding
in the light
of the city at night.
People have gone to bed and left
the lights burning
in the streets.

The girl lies
on the balcony
on her back. She stares
up through the lights
toward stars she can't see.

The maple leaves
hang like hands
in the light, in the dark
around her. They hang
upside-down, like her, upside-down
on her back.
The leaves turn
at the wrist
in the breeze, raise
a soft applause
for the stars hidden
backstage, for the people
sleeping in the wings.

A soft applause, while
the girl
lies on her back on the balcony,
before the lights go out, before
the light comes up,
before another day

begins and the girl, watching
from the balcony, moves
through the door
into the waking house,
walks down the hall
to her bed and falls
through dreams
into the hands of the maple.

The girl is walking
down a street lined
with trees, their branches
the skin of a sea
overhead, waves
of light brushing tides
on the sidewalk, and leaving
foam on her curious brow.
She stops
her walking through watery
leaves and light and turns
her head to the side, as though some current
has changed and caught her
by the chin, but she is just turning
away from the sound of traffic
and toward a choir
of nesting birds,
or she stops
and collapses
to her knees, as though the tide
had taken her
down with its weight, smoothed
itself along her frame, but she is just bending
away from the height of strolling neighbours
and searching for the company
of smaller, gentler bodies, emerging
from grass blades
in the boulevard,
or she stops
and lets her hand float
out, as though a wave
had buoyed it
along on its crest, but she is just reaching
away from the air
and toward the sea
she finds reflected around her
in the skin of leaves.

In the forest, the girl can't help but remember
how everything fights
to reach its arms up
to the sky, everything stands, waiting
for the sky to reach down like a parent,
pick it up, take it away, but
the parent never comes.

In the forest, the girl remembers
how everything lies down
when it gives
up, bodies topple to make space
for others, to make space
for nothing, no one
can explain why
bodies tire and dry.

In the forest, she remembers
how everything speaks, leaves
a constant chatter
in the cold
wind, a constant warm whisper
in the heat, branches creaking
like bones, a skeletal voice,
a voice from deep inside.

How everything shelters something beneath
itself, how no one stands with no one
under its arms.

How seeds fall
from everything, and without the girl
being aware, things blossom
up, she plants
herself wherever she stands.

How could she not
remember, in the forest, how could she stand
beneath so many trees, saplings
at her knees, seeds
under her heels, how

could she stand there and not remember
her arms are branches
    her toes are roots
        her hair is leaves
           her skin, bark
her thoughts are sap rising, rising through her.

*T*his prairie fits the girl
as the sky fits the horizon,
covers it with its body, all
day, all night and never
lets go. You see exactly
how they lie, press, together.

When the birds wake, they fill
the sky with their songs, trails
of bubbles, crossing, floating
away. You can't
catch them. And sometimes,
when the birds sing
all at once, the sky fills
with coloured ribbons, loosely
entangled, rippling.
They cannot be drawn
straight or apart.

This prairie fits the girl
as the sky fits the morning
songs of birds, shows her
the trick of itself, land
and air, one
long line she can trace with her finger.

The girl watches a sparrow
stand
at the end of a dry stick, the stick
dip
slow and smooth with the sparrow's weight,
and the sparrow
flit
up just as the stick
breaks and
falls.

The girl watches white butterflies
dive
and cross
paths, hover
three feet apart,
dive
and cross again
and again, until the wind brushes them away.

The girl watches a bank of purple hyacinths
sway
their bodies toward her like a line of dancers,
lean
their bodies away, graceful, perfect,
all afternoon they dance and do not tire.

The girl is trying to think of a language.
It sounds like air
the tongue shapes
against the roof of the mouth,
against the inside
of the cheeks, the lips. It sounds
like mouths and cheeks and lips
of the wind, blowing through the tall grass, blowing
through her head.

    The scratch of a woodchuck's nails
on the dry logs in the woodpile.

    Two of them now
sitting on the woodpile,
scratching.

The girl is watching. The girl can
watch and move however she wants, so long
as she doesn't make sounds
she already knows.

    The scratch of the woodchuck's nails, it
comes to her like
the lips of the wind
up the hill, through the grass.

The girl's mouth is a
magnet, an
undertow, the
pupil of an eye drawing
everything through itself.

When the girl opens her mouth
to ask, dark O,
she is saying,
there is a space in here
which needs to be filled. She
steadies the magnet,
begins the motion of the undertow,
opens her eyelids, says,
everything
I look at rushes into me, says,
whenever I open my mouth to ask,
any sound
left hanging in air
will find its way to my belly.

*A*nd the girl's mouth must move
through and around all words,
must gently kiss
itself, lick the insides of its own
body if the words are to come out,
how intimate, this kissing,
how private. No wonder she
speaks so softly.

Ophelia's brush-stroked mouth, open slightly
forever, no longer
needs words, but the girl's
lips coax
flower petals in,
a spoonful of rain,
drop in notes of a bird song one by one.

Ophelia, hanging
silent, under glass,
the girl watches your mouth.
When she says your name,
she kisses you.

The girl holds wonder
in her body, she does
not let it move
to her head, it would
get harder and harder there, like a skull.

Wonder can only preserve
itself
in the suppleness
of skin.

She holds it,
immediate
in everything she touches, in
    Ophelia's mouth,
    a raven's wing,
    the dye from oyster shells, in
        a muddy boot,
        gusts of breeze,
        a heartbeat under her hand,
    the things that are new
        and things already familiar, the girl's skin
falls
into wonder every time
she touches, if
she holds it there, if
she keeps everything
she loves in her body.

They say Ophelia sang
as she drowned. As though she didn't know
opening your mouth underwater
lets death in. She traded
a few mournful notes, quivering in air, for a mouthful
of something she could swallow.

Ophelia, what if the girl threw away
the spoon, forgot about filling you
with water from the sky, what if she reached
past your lips and pulled those colourful petals
from your tongue, the way a mother clears her baby's throat
of something she might choke on, what if
the girl kept all the notes of that bird song
cupped in her hand.

What would you say
to her then, Ophelia. What could you
say, but, *Water*, but,
Swallow what you drown in.

Imagine

    Ophelia, floating
    like an island
    in the bodies of oceans and seas, so many
        arms holding her up
        for breath,
            watery fingers tapping rhythms
            on her sandy knees, in measure
            with crashing swirling songs,
                backs of hands held
                to her forehead,
                taking her temperature,
                wringing water onto her burning skin.

And imagine

    the Assiniboine breaking
    on the rocks, and the girl
    on the bank, watching
    herself move toward the water,
    naked, finally entering
    the river she walks beside each day.

Purple Flowers

*L*et me tell you how you were
　　desired. You were desired
as something inside.
An unborn child.
An adopted child,
A child who died long ago.

　　You were desired
as a painting desires its painter,

as the painter desires the muse.

　　You were desired
as something far away,
the first footfalls on the moon,

as something possible,
but elusive, a cure
for disease.

Something simple, but unlikely,
rain, falling
in a desert.

　　You were desired
as the sky
by trees, holding their arms up
to its light.

As the night
by stars.

Like the desiring stars,
I was desperate for you to see me
and I was desperate not
to fall.

Warm summer nights, I will miss
warm summer nights on the screened-in balcony,
air blowing gently through, jazz
blowing gently through, and an old lava lamp
in constant motion, slow
sensuous writhing and rippling, the postures
we move through, but can't see.

In the morning, you will call, tell me
of purple flowers that opened in the dark,
we were surrounded
by their silent blooming, as though
this gentle celebration of a balcony,
of wine and jazz and life's contortions,
was just what they were
waiting for, those purple flowers.

Walking home,
everything in halves, you walk me half-way
at half-light, birds half in song,
half a bottle of wine in each of our stomachs,
half a face of the moon watching down.

I wonder at all these halves,
such a full night, so full with life,
and me so filled with you.

When he goes to Thailand
    she will give him thick new socks, so that
        when he walks down the roads, disturbs
            scorpions sleeping in the ruts,
nothing will crawl in
    the holes his big toes cut, nothing will harm him
        cruelly as the sting of the scorpion, nothing will
            poison his skin, his blood.

She will give him socks when he goes to Thailand
    because she wants him to walk
        down those dusty roads, walk
            between fields at night, rice growing
the colour of the moon, she wants him
    to carry pails of water, swinging
        from the ends of a stick he balances
            across his shoulders like a long straight promise.

She wants him to walk behind the carts
    bumping their way to the market, fruits and vegetables,
        fabric and tin, piled high inside, she wants him
            to walk behind and pick up a bamboo fan
that jostles out, wave it above his wet chest
    when the sun is farthest away
        from this country he left behind, and think
            of her body still resting here, in the dark.

These are the things my mouth does in
the dark, these months without
your body. My mouth

sips at breeze, gusting
through the screen,
like mouthfuls of cool wine
you tip to my lips, my mouth

swallows silence down into my belly, you not here
to kiss my sleeping lips closed, my mouth

hums quiet tunes, breathing
in, the melody, breathing out, the harmony, my mouth

sings a song for you, La dee daaa, dee daaa, dee daaa,
I laa-ve you, my mouth

laughs across the pillow, notes and
shadows where your hair should be, my mouth

screams, red, splitting the dark
into your absent outstretched arms, my mouth

sucks on my skin, wanting it
to be yours, my mouth

 talks to itself, says, not much longer till
 you taste him,

whispers,
this is what I'm doing, these months
without your body, whispers,
this is how I survive
without you, in the dark.

*Y*ou could love me from a distance, as you love time, never
encountering her, but always
expecting her, half-past eight, quarter to midnight,

always calling her
different names for her different faces,
moods, ways she moves
her body in the light
and the dark, through seasons.

Just when you think you know her, she
slips from around your wrist.
You turn a corner, find her
watching from the shadows. Look behind,
she disappears over a hill.

You kiss her open mouth,
but she won't kiss back, her lips
like air, you touch her skin,
but you can't tell
her age, her shape, her body
is water under your hands.

You call her up, and believe
you hear her
singing on the line, through static.
You mail her letters, and they come back
sealed, though you think
you smell her
when you open them.

You wake in the night, feel her
trailing her fingertips up your chest,
swinging her hair down into your face,
but she is just after
your heartbeat, your breath.

Do not love me
from a distance
as you love time.
When you say,
always,
expect my name
unchanging in your mouth,
my presence
clear as your voice.

*H*e plugs the ears
of their relationship
so he can hear it from inside.

He listens to her voice,
like clay pressed
through the receiver.

He listens to her whispers,
soft sounds that might just be
the wind blowing through her hair,
bedsheets rustling on the clothesline,
fingers leafing through a stack of mail.

He listens to her
skin breathing, hears
the silence
resting
between the whimper of the mole on her thigh,
and the hush of the freckle on her breast.

He listens and listens
but thinks
he can't hear
how they sound from inside,
for the noise
of her scratching pen.

Beyond wishing, she wishes
you could feel her, like the poem
she is. If you could
feel her that way, she would
have so many syllables, rhymes,
a beautiful sound on your tongue, a
rhythm, you would always know
where she's moving next, but
never know just how
she'd take you
there. She would
wrap herself around you,
like the poem she is. You would rest
inside her, like breath.

*T*o come back from an afternoon
walk along the Assiniboine,

wash my hair
with marigold flowers and thyme,

put on a clean white cotton T-shirt,

eat a plum,
skin the colour of dark wine, flesh
the colour of grapefruit,
but sweeter,

to watch the sun fade from the street,

to sit with my sketchbook's blank page
and a sharpened pencil,

to feel Brahms' clarinet, cello, piano
moving through bars
of notes, leaving,
returning to each other
as three parts of my self,

to know that somewhere you move
as a fourth part of me, the part
that saves me from these words...

What else? What else can there be
in this moment? What else can there be,
but the silence surrounding it all?

*W*hat a

     surprise to find
you, like finding myself standing
inside the foundation of an abandoned house
after I'd left the paths at the park,
scrub and earth keeping the blank pages
of concrete between them
like a secret, a

     surprise,
the stairs that used to lead to a door,
an empty frame filled
with sky and stepping
up is like stepping toward
you,
and what a

     surprise, finding
these words in my head,
more doors opening onto the sky,
more stairs
barely visible, sudden shifts of light,
carrying me up to other rooms, and
layered voices calling down
from landings and hallways,
beckoning me away
for a while, summoning me
to a lost afternoon,

then leading me back
to you.

I love you
furiously. I love you
like the dancer spinning
in an empty room,
leaping   collapsing
on an oak floor,
in a path of sunlight.

I love you
like the sculptor moving her hands
over marble, knowing
of a centre she will never carve, so
cold   solid   silent.

I love you
like the gardener
with dirt on her knees,
purple flowers in her hair,
creeping-thyme tucked under her tongue,

like the carpenter sanding pine,
fragrance of wood on her skin all day,

like the potter warming clay
with the heat of her palms,

like the musician in a rainstorm.

I love you
in so many layers, in so much space,
in skies of white paper,
I love you
off this land, past these stars,
like the poet who takes you with her.

$\mathcal{I}$ would walk with you
through the afternoon, wait
with you, would surround
you with my body.

When the peaceful dark came down
like a mother returning,
I would let you go, gently
into the night.

I've been holding you like this
for hundreds of years. We are old
together, like the sky and the moon.

The Daughters of Silence

*L*et me
disturb you. Let's do it
like this. I'll tell you

about the cat in heat
who came home
limping, the skin on her nose
scraped off, her body leaking blood
and semen. I'll tell you
that's what it is to be fucked
if you're a cat, I'll ask you
aren't we animals? Aren't we animals
too? I'll tell you

about the husband in heat
who came home with a fresh lemon loaf, he
fed it to his family, asked them how they liked it, he
didn't poison them, if that's what you're thinking, unless,
let me ask you, is it poison, eating the baking
of a lover you didn't know he had? I'll tell you

what you thought I might tell you. I'll tell you
about the bus, driving way too fast
down highways in Colombia, I'll tell you
how a man said from the backseat,
that guy's gonna kill someone, and
not ten miles later we looked out the window, saw her
lying facedown, just like they say, a bag of rags, her
long grey hair, spread like a fan, her
basket of vegetables, scattered like colourful petals by wind,
the night too dark to see how the blood flowed, to tell you
what it looked like, maybe a brown bedspread, maybe
the woman's sticky shadow. I'll tell you

about the three by four by six foot box
sitting at the side of the road in the steam of the
gutter, that when I passed one morning, they kept
coming out and coming out, this house for
a family of five. You think it's funny, this was
not a circus trick, and it's not
magic that their mother keeps her husband
alive with milk from her breasts. Any
new mother could do it. I'll tell you

about arriving to do CPR, and finding the victim has
no head, about

a little girl, so well-trained she
hikes down her diapers so
daddy can touch, about

the child in the playground, yelling
from the top of the slide that
all the other kids are going
to burn in hell, about

the father, who whispers, moments before death,
I was a good parent, your mom and I raised two good kids,
about his daughter looking down into his eyes, mouthing,
You were a shit. A thoughtless, deceitful shit,
turning, walking out the door. I'll tell you

this, I'll tell you so much more, and
then
I'll ask, what
        do you see what
                do you hear what
                        do you smell, do you taste,
I'll ask you,
what, tell me, what,
tell me.

This is the one who strangled
my mother. I found him
with his hands around her throat, her face
turning purple, when I ran
from the shower, towel clutched
around me, suds in my hair, not
to see what was happening, not
even to help, I just ran
when I heard her desperate sucking-for-air, his
dizzy rage, and the bed
slamming and slamming against the floor, the wall, just him
slamming her body again and again
onto the bed, I ran
from the shower to their room, just because
that's where my feet took me. Just as
now my feet have taken me
out of that house of screaming and silence,
but my feet cannot take me
out of this house of my head, my body, what they remember.
This one was strangling my mother
with his hands, the hands he loves
to tell me held my naked bum
when I was born, a little bum
small enough to fit in one of those huge
hands. He carries me.
He carries me still.

A woman crying and crying, a voice echoing
off the surface of a place
inside her, a place
I haven't heard from for a long long time.
I remember this voice from the years

when her bones went missing.
She couldn't stand, couldn't sit, her body
was jelly inside soft skin, so heavy and slippery

I couldn't hold her up alone.

And there was this voice
from someplace far away, wailing, wailing
the same pitch, like a bow gliding

across the A-string of a violin and,
at rhythmic intervals, maybe to the count
of her weakening

pulse, she screamed
    I just want to die
        (*die*, trailing down and down,
           back to where it came from far inside)
        I just want to die,

her teeth chattering, keeping a staccato time, tears

like so many mourning
notes sliding from the black mouth
of an oboe.

*M*om, the tiny blue flowers I picked
to send you, they will never be missed
from the carpets of blue their sisters have

laid across the floor of the park
where I walk beside the river, they will never be
missed from the blankets the sister-flowers lay

across the cool feet of the trees.
I see the flowers, blue women, pushed
silently up, bent quietly down, delicate

throats, voices muffled in the ground, and immediately,
I miss you, almost as much as I imagine you
may have missed yourself, these thirty years.

We could always make you raise your voice
if we tried to touch your hair, and
I creep into the blanket of flowers,

pull two out of the ground, like flowers
growing from your skin,
but this time, you do not shoo me away,

you raise your voice to sing out clear and
blue as the faces of flowers. I
put your singing voice carefully

in my pocket, those two blue flowers,
their petals a handful of musical notes
in my palm. The flowers lie

on my table now, waiting
to be mailed, and you are singing to me,
all afternoon. You'll open the envelope, find

two dried flowers, I will send to you, two
silhouettes of the voice
you left me.

*W*hat can be so heavy inside
that it holds you
back from the things you love,
like a paperweight, keeping the sheets
of yourself from flying
free when the wind comes by to collect them.

You drag it with you
like a ball chained
to your kidneys, your liver, like an anchor
that keeps you docked, that will not
let you sail.

It feels like the night
on your shoulders, you stagger
under a dark sky, pressing you
deeper and deeper into the ground
as you try to walk, to run,
as you try to simply stand.

Your arms tire with carrying it,
a dictionary, a set of encyclopedias,
you want to write it out of you,
but you are hanging
on to each word you've learned.

And the mountains are dead, but still
they know that the earth is warmer, more alive
than the sun. Look

at their foreheads, their shoulders, look
at the snow that will not melt, though they reach

closer to the sun than we let our thoughts go, look

how they warm their feet in the earth.

The spruce, the pines try to cover this death
with life, try to make something of it,
as we do, as I cover the dead
with poems, as I lay pages over dead bodies
in sheets, in shrouds. As though we could

miss it, as though we could pretend
it was something else, all around us, sucking
at the earth, filling the sky, like mountains,

mountains reaching for heat they can't find.

She is screaming
and screaming and screaming for something
that has no name.
                    She screams,

                         look
at this woman lying face-down-dead in the street.

And everyone passes by,
whistling.

       She is singing
and singing and singing a tune
that has no melody.
                    She sings,

                         look
at the quetzal rising from a bush,
red roses growing out of concrete.

But no one notices,
they are trimming their hedges, edging the lawn.

                    She sighs,

they don't want words from under the ground
or words from a far-away sky.
They just want words that will blow the dust around.

*L*et's be honest about the dark, let's not
pretend the moon only shines
on some parts of the earth, that
certain citizens carry stars
in their pockets, that these
fingers are rays of the sun.

No matter

how the steel wraps around
you and the glass you sit behind, how
these frame the night outside, or
what name is printed on the sign
at the nearest corner
in this grid of concrete and lights
that control when you move,
when you stand
still, when you curse,
no matter

what lines your pocket, silk, suede,
or what's trapped inside that expensive
hunting sack, plastic cards that make money
spit from tight-lipped mouths, silver
keys, pierced
through the feet and bound
together, slaves that open
doors to houses, offices, cottages, hotel rooms,
cars, spa lockers, and safety
deposit boxes,
no matter

what encircles your fingers,
tiny shackles
of hammered gold, glossy
paints hardening on your nails
like the blood of the poor, alluring
scents you rub into your wrists,
no matter

what ensnares you
on the ground, every sky
is the sky I'm looking at now.

…What's between
the sky and the dark
space inside….

These layers of entrapment
we can point at and hold
out in front of us like warning flags, or
flags of surrender, and
these intangible layered words,
dressings made out of words, and me

not knowing
how to peel them back
like the white skin from my bones,
how to pry my own bones open.

*H*ow does it go
in those hot, hot countries, in those hot
languages, syllables flaring off the tongue, fiery
    as Aguardiente,
        as the hips of Salsa dancers, colourful
            as Guatemalan *traje*.

                Where do you find the dark
with all that fire, with all that colour
burning your skin.
    With bullets burning
      everyone's ears,
        hunger burning
        the insides of stomachs,
          wet feet burning
          paths into concrete, and
lies lies lies
hanging
    from buildings,
        overpasses,
          busracks,
and burning
like my white skin, in effigy.

I am a white
ragdoll passing through.
    I have diamonds
    for eyes and straw
    for understanding.
        I have a dove
        for a heart,
        but it doesn't know where to land,
I want
the dark, yet in those countries, I'm
white white white.

I once rocked children
—*los vegetales*, they called them, the vegetables—
in a hospital
in Antigua, Guatemala.
They reached out their arms
when I arrived in the mornings,
shouted to me
in Spanish
in Quiché
in Cakchiquel
in all the languages
God has forgotten.
They stunk of shit and amoebas,
their matching green pyjamas soaked
with urine, and they rolled
their heads, their eyes,
away from the wall toward the sun.
I talked in broken words
in a broken voice,
I leaned on their chairs,
pushed them around the courtyard,
I lifted them out of straps
and stumbled
where they pointed, so they could look
into rooms they had never seen.
The blind one couldn't see, of course,
but I let him play with a camera,
and I have the picture.

I wonder how they are.
I wonder if they've grown too big
to be lifted.
I try to stay small,
to remember their
small arms, rocking
me.

The little soldier carries a gun,
he is in the square, surrounded
by flowers and children.

He is dressed in coarse green,
a grassy fabric,
the colour of things that grow.

Surrounded by growing
flowers and children, the little
soldier.

Little girl with rubber boots
    half-way to your knees, I first
    see you, peeking out from behind
    your mother's skirt, making
    little-girl faces at me. You are
    a flashback, a memory
    of fourteen years ago,
            of dark hair swinging in a pony-tail,
                of shiny brown eyes scrunching
                and rolling around, grabbing
                other people's eyes and dropping
                them, childishly, with one blink,
                    of a belief in games of pretend
                    and in myself,
    I watch you, trying to remember
    how I would have hopped
    from log to thick puddle, would have thrown
    stones at chickens and chased
    after them, wanting to show everyone
    how fast I could run, how carefree.

Little girl with rubber boots
    half-way to your knees, I last
    see you, sitting on an old *pila*,
    knees tucked up, away
    from sewage water that seeps
    through your cardboard walls.
    You won't smile at me, won't
    play anymore, as I wave, as I
    pull away in the van.

*S*panish, so fluid,
it rushes right to the centre,
it lets the darkness out,

a flood. And
everything floats
by, Caesar's guitar,

Rosa's *buñuelos*,
Mareceli's long black hair,
Carlos' soccer ball,

Marco Tulio's shifty stride and
two-year-old Juan Camilo,
flexing his muscles and showing off

his red underwear.
Luzdy, you float by,
and Martha, you

float by, and Penson, you float, standing
on a table waving your arms, reading me
Spanish poetry in the office.

The boy sketching faces for money,
and the woman with scars covering her skin,
and the man who followed me when I was alone.

The Puddle Girl floats by at the end
of the flood. She wouldn't then, but now
she waves goodbye.

In my dreams, when they speak Spanish,
I always put my head down and cry.

I want to sit in the cathedral
of El Peten jungle, I want

I want the toucan, the quetzal,
decorated saints, I want

I want the Usumacinta river before me,
its never-ending grace, I want

every leaf on every *jacaranda* hanging
like promises from the light.

And I want all the scorpions
dead as Good Friday, never rising up again.

Who will rise up
for more than the lifetime it takes to make
all the mud dry
under the Puddle Girl's feet?

I put my head down, I am
crying in the mud.

The Mayan city in Tikal
　　　still stands.
They drained their daughters' blood to keep
　　　the sun from dying.
They wear its darkness in their skin.

And me here,
building cities

out of white

paper that crumples

in one frail fist, that melts
when left out in an evening's rain,

a dead dove in my heart,
collapsing.

       Am I
sacrificing
the daughters of silence for nothing?

Juan Manuel, I come back from your country
with threads the colours of Guatemalan *traje*,
woven through my thoughts.
My Guatemala, scattered
blocks, quickly sewn together
by the calloused hands of black-haired women.

And now, my head all stitched through
with bits of Guatemala, not
making any sense against a background
of North American fabrics, I
pull away at the faintest pin-prick.

Many North Americans have told me,
It's not your fault.
This is how the world is.
You have to get on with your life.

But I needed words
from a dark mouth
that marries letters
of the alphabet, B's and V's,
that makes everything happen
clean at the front,
that can't swallow the real
words, or
hide them inside
behind lies.

You tell me,
It's not your fault.
The world was like this before you were born.
Do what you can where you are.

And you tell me
there is always sadness
in my eyes,
even when I smile.

Maybe it's that all my life I've woken
in the dark. It has managed to squeeze
in, and the bright Guatemalan colours, embroidered
dancers, flowers, quetzals, they
don't fool me, there is something far
more
sinister holding
our continents together.

Juan Manuel, you say
you were a painter in your past life,
that no one paid attention to your work,
and now you have another chance to make
them see, or maybe
they loved you,
you were very famous
then, and now you must struggle,
it's part of your work this time around.

I say,
is it part of your work, this time, to watch
your friends disappear,
is it part of your work to see how they turn
up dead? Is it your work to find
you are next on the list, that they
have a spot marked out for you,
in a rose garden like Romero,
you can lie there forever, face
down in petals, feeding your dark
blood to the roots.

And is it part of your work, Juan,
to hold a woman who can barely hold herself
in, remembering
how they raped her, remembering her son
ripped open, left alone, fading
into some other place, darkening
the concrete.

Juan, in paint, you see
how things can change. You show me

a candle whose flame becomes a dove, escaping
barbed wire, a tree whose leaves
become quetzals, rising
from the jungle, a woman whose long back
becomes the flux of the sea, shifting
sleepily against a sheet
of sand, a girl whose almond eyes
are butterfly-wings, as she flies
she stares
at me.

Convince me.
Convince me that you didn't mean to
rip our insides out, that you didn't know
you had our tendons and nerves
wound around your fingers, our intestines
slipping from your hands, knotted, swollen, bruised
like worms drowned after a rain, or dying slowly
after someone steps on half their body, convince me
you didn't taste our blood
in your mouth as you spit out our skin,
didn't notice our hair still
caught in your teeth.
Convince me, with all this ripped
up flesh, this blood and vomiting
and screaming that will not end,
convince me that
you committed this massacre
in all innocence.

Or did you think there was a doctor?
Did you think there was a surgeon
who could figure out
which parts belonged to whom, sort them
into piles, stitch everyone back together,
an intricate operation, with so many
stretchers, with needles
and suture thread filling the air,
like a net cast into the empty sky.

I was murdered,
I was murdered in that life.

They buried me.
They scrubbed their hands clean.

An Open Hand

I am certain women went to lakes
to birth their babies, I am certain
they entered the water to their chests,
that each knew how the rocks lay,
knew how to lay themselves on the rocks
in the water.

I am certain of the water,
how I lay myself in it to birth
anything how the water eases
everything out of me, how
everywhere I go, I take myself
down to the water. I can

birth myself
into a city, enter the streets
quietly from the east, when the lights are off
and everyone's asleep. I can

birth words onto the page, whole poems
wet and dripping, crying for me
to show them how to live
in a dry and fragmented world. I can

birth you against my thighs, I am
the beach laid down and spread
beneath you, you are the tide, I can
send you back out to yourself in new rhythms.

I can birth fear and anger and grief and pain, all those
burning states, those things we keep
sticking our arms through, things we can't
wrestle down once and for all, I can
take them from you, swallow them
into my chest, I can
birth them through me, not
down to the ground, or into the air, I can
birth them away,
they are gone.

Every day, I go to the lake, I go
to rivers and seashores and waterfalls. Every day
I go with the women to the birthing waters, and
the world passes
through me.

*S*itting on this bank
on Manitoulin Island
summer after summer
since I was
a child, sitting here
since before I was
born, swimming
in my mother's belly,
I feel every June July August
that has passed for 26 years.
     A place so familiar,
just sitting brings back
years indecipherable
as reeds standing together in the silt,
crows calling from the leafy branches,
ripples in the creek where the water breaks
over the stones.
     This bank, so familiar,
Lake Huron runs through my veins,
sand settles around my pupils.
Crabgrass and wild flowers of every colour
fall from my mouth.

*L*eaving everything to hang open,
as the edge of the world
hangs open, she has to watch
where she walks or she might step off.

She is stepping off the edge
of the world, there
across the North Channel, just over
the other side of the mountains
that lie asleep on their backs, tired
as the settlers moving rock
after rock to clear
the land, tired as the dark ones
who first paddled through,
who paddle away and away.

Across the North Channel, on the other side
of the mountains, don't be surprised
if you find the tired ones sleeping.
Mindemoya, the Old Woman, sleeps
above Grandpa's grave, she sleeps
in the heart
of this Island.

Mindemoya is tired, she rises
from the centre, moves
to the edge. Mindemoya
steps over the hills to the north
of the channel, she
steps off the edge
of the world and I go with her.

A woman carries me
　　with her as she dives
　　head-first
　　　　into a bed
　　　　of blue sheets,
wrapping around her face and shoulders,
　　rippling as she falls and falls,
　　she could fall forever,
　　　　never ground her
　　　　skin in silt or sand.
She brushes past fish, slivers of the moon
　　scattered and swimming in oceans and seas,
　　past kelp, Medusa's hair,
　　　　a thousand snaky tongues smelling
　　　　whoever comes near,
this kelp can freeze you,
　　tangle you in as you pass
　　and hold you underwater,
　　　　turn your curious body
　　　　to stone.
The woman who dives into water
　　returns to me on the shore,
　　drops of lake a fine sweat on her skin,
　　　　slivers of the moon caught in her teeth,
　　　　strands of kelp wound dangerously around her wrists.
She tells me she thought of me while she swam.

She learned to surrender to the water
way before she learned

to surrender to herself.
She gives herself to the water and

it takes her away
in pieces, gives her back, whole.

She has taken
to imagining

women, going to the water
together. They stand

naked, under waterfalls.
Together they give themselves

over, then I
come back

to you, I come back to you,
dripping wet, I surrender.

You are dark
and strands of your dark hair fall
to weave themselves with grass blades.
Your feet move across the ground
like mothers' hands
patting the backs of babies.
You know fire so carefully
it sparks from your fingernails
and jumps to the birch bark you peel
back with your heat.
The drum softens
and warms when you rub
its skin before you
start to hit, gives
the pulse of your fingers back
to the air, where
everyone can feel you.
Your grandparents came to this Island
years ago, more than anyone
can count, more than the number
of sticks I could line up
in crossed-out fives
after a day
of gathering and breaking.
What were their names, and
how do you pronounce them,
how did you fit your mouth around
the clean Ojibwa syllables?
How did you throw your voice
across a deep laugh
that fell from your open
mouth into the hands
of strangers
who did not understand? My relatives
came to this Island, they
have blue eyes, the tops of thin pools,
and hair lighter
than my skin. But ——— (I don't
know your name,
though I'm calling you),

I am dark. I
am the night,
like you, we are dark
selves who can draw each other
into holding, resting, dreaming,
and other thick acts.
We can hear blue pools,
without having to carry them
in our eyes. You pull me
out of opaque dusk, out
of my half-dark night, and
into the air that's so still
I forget morning
will come waving
her arms through the trees.
You feel what it's like to stand
beside me, then look
at my face and say, *healer*.
You feel what it's like to stand
with the animals and the colours,
the stars, the sand, sounds
that fit like zipper-teeth, and they sink
into me when I lock
up my words, when I follow
your eyes, let the wind blow
through my ears. You whisper
the histories thin
pool-eyes can't pour
down, the quiet secrets tucked
behind and beneath. You show
me how to let my blood run out
of my feet and into the ground,
you play nasal music, charm
my hair to twist around yours,
like Island paintings,
our blood, our hair, runs, twists
through black sand that ground
itself out of rock, layers
below flowers that rise and sway
from earth that has never felt
the sun, that's dark
like us.

The sunset is

a woman, dressed
in her purple skin. Always

between light and dark, she is

there, reminding you
that you too move between light

and dark. That's where you find
yourself, brilliant, fading.

I don't ask
that you break the sky open, show me
    the floating cave
        where the purple woman lives.
                        I don't ask
that you grab her by the hair, by the toes, pull her
    down, unconscious, so I can see her close up, so I can
        put my mouth to hers and learn
            who will resuscitate whom.
                        I don't ask
that you paint your body
    with the juice of African violets,
        with the dye Lydia made from oyster shells,
            that you grow your hair long, or speak
                in a voice high as clouds.

I don't ask
anything of you, except
that you know where I am,
that you know I'd fall
like purple rain from the sky
if you broke it open,
if I asked you to break me open.
My body is the cave where she lives.

When she opens her hands and holds
her palms up, anything can happen.

>Rain can begin to fall from the sky
>>for the first time in weeks, thirsty
>>for the earth, desperate
>>to soak itself into another body.

>Lightning can shock down, singe her
>>there, in the centre of the palm, burning
>>a target for some pounder of nails.

>The air can begin to spin
>>if she moves her open hands in a circle.
>>She can make a tornado, blow
>>everything up and around and around
>>and away.

>Sparrows and orioles can land,
>>weave nests, fasten them
>>to her fingers, leave
>>their eggs to hatch in her warmth.

>Children swinging from branches can dip
>>their toes down, smear dirt
>>and crumbs of bark on the heels
>>of her palms, so she won't
>>forget them.

>Ghosts can sprinkle
>>words, drop thousands of them, wet
>>and black, their images drying
>>on her skin, even after
>>the wind blows the words away.

>A purple-bodied woman can reach
>>her tongue out of the sky, lick
>>her palms until she's clean, easy, until
>>all her fingerprints are smoothed and gone.

And, if you watch carefully,
when she opens her hands and holds them up,
things can fly out. Soft sounds, bright colours,
leave the veins in her wrists and fingertips
and enter the air like a cloud of butterflies.

She is filled with everything
she has seen, touched,
and these things, they are
flowing out. See
what it is now, the
shell of an insect crumbling to dust,
the purple sunset
soaking into the ground, a white
dandelion puff. You
breathe on me, and I
disconnect at the centre, float
away. Who knows where
or how we flower
again,
                except there will be
                water and dark earth and sun,
                there will be sky.

Floating Ophelia

*O*phelia, there was a time when I looked
in a mirror
to find
a drowning woman. There was a time
when I threw myself
down on its glass and opened my hands.
Everything floated
from me like loosed flowers on a current.
I was heavy, pressed
into a reflection
of someone I might have been, and every day
I'd missed as I lay, immersed
in surfaces
of night, though I could hear
night's deeper body
calling. Now I look
at you, open
and opening
on the wall before me, an entire
garden giving its body
over to the ecstasy of pushing, spreading, unfolding. Today
it is late June, but I know it is
Spring and you are only beginning,
my feet planted under this desk, like roots
in rich soil. You are only beginning to speak
to me across this garden
we share, wafting words. If I
don't forget to breathe
deeply, I will draw them
inside myself, definite, illusive,
the scent
of pansy, scent of sage.

And there is no glass.
There is no glass between us.

These flowers float, a final
stretching open,
a final celebration, final
wilt and decay. They drift
around Ophelia's blind
fingertips,
       some purple as a woman's untouched
       desire,
          some blue as her babies
          never born.
              Some yellow as the coat of guilt
              inside her cheeks, words
              spooned in and sucked on, rotting.
                 Some pink as moments
                 of distraction.
                    Red as loss,
                       orange as racing
                       nightmares, and
                           white
                           as everything
                           forgotten.

Ophelia and I whisper
to each other, *don't forget
green, pushing up
from the ground and drawing down
the sun. Remember green, the growing,
urgent and audacious as seasons surely
numbed and overtaken.*

You say you've never seen anger
light as the floating hand
of a drowned woman, you've never seen it pale
as a dead woman's face, or empty
as her open mouth, anger
empty as the mouths of the dead,
and you've never seen eyes so blind
with anger, they do not move, do not
blink. You see

how it concentrates
in her hips, sinks
them to the floor
of the brook, her waist held
between thighs
of rock and encircled
by the fine arms of algae.

                    But her chest rises
up, Ophelia's chest rises up, up
and out of the water.

                    A vulture
might sweep a swath of sky
clean with its wings and tear
a scrap from her dress, pluck
the nipple from her breast, dig
for an artery, a ventricle,
for death. The vulture might
become a dove, might
carry a piece of her
in its beak, fly her
back to the boat still docked in the harbour

and sing,
I have found it, there
is dry land
in this body, there is something
not sunk, there is
hope.

*L*ike a mermaid, they say,
Ophelia's shimmering dress, silver
scales and no feet.
Haven't they heard
how bud turns to blossom and worm
to butterfly. Haven't they heard
even mermaids grow legs.
But instead of learning to walk
on the land, this one will fly, will dangle
her toes free in the air, and the voice
that lured love to its end in the sea
will call love out of its many bodies
and up to the sky, she will sing stronger and louder
as she flies, contralto
luring love out
to itself, luring love back
to its beginning.

Everyone thinks Ophelia's dead.
Forget the woman

who stood on the edge
of a steep bank, lassoed
in vines and garlands, arms

filled with flowers
she loved and broke
at the throat because she needed them to speak
as her last breath, held
out to the world.

Sometimes a woman knows
her only chance is to hold
her own voice, wrap
the speaking world around her
and lie floating in its arms.

So forget the woman who stood at the edge
of a steep bank and
threw
her body into the world's speaking arms, forget
the one who died as the world held her, rocked her
in the current
        of a brook
in the shade
        of a willow,
forget that
woman everyone thinks is dead.

Open your eyes
wider
and see
the one who hangs
above the girl's desk

is alive as one

who reaches out
as colour through a pane of glass.

*O*phelia is getting up, leaving
the soaked heavy dress behind
like a useless skin, she flies
naked and free, up from the canvas.

I see her pale toes dangling, disappearing
as she crosses out of the frame,
I see the stems of the flowers
she has gathered back together
in her strong, sure fist, they raise her
into the sky, like a bouquet
of balloons, and

there is a shower of bright petals
blowing across my desk, they look like
poems, but believe me, they are
the petals of wild flowers.

It's like that river flowing past. It didn't ask
to leave the mountains,
to pour into the sea. It didn't ask
for us to walk beside it, creating
a second river
of dust, to trace it
with ink onto maps, to build
walls against it, to fall
in love with its constant motion, its changing
personalities. It didn't ask

to understand better than we ever will
how to flow through this place, how to
accept its own motion, its freedom
from drowning in itself.

It didn't ask for anything.

I am slowly learning, sometimes
returning to where I started and beginning
to learn again,
not to ask,
but to lay my body down, like a river.

Acknowledgements

George Amabile, thank you for accompanying me on this mysterious adventure. You have been a most faithful advisor, teacher, guide…. Thank you for gently watering me, for lovingly moving me in and out of the sun. Although you never appear in these poems in reference, you exist throughout them because you nurtured these words, and me.

Thank you also: Lisa Seymour, for offering a safe space to speak, embracing and permeating me with your powerful kindness, being a mirror-who-takes-me-inside-herself, seeing me as I am in each moment and enabling me to see myself anew; and Strong Eagle, for being my companion, walking and resting alongside me, caring for the whole circle of me with the whole circle of you. Thank you: Rochelle Martin and Ron Dick, for inspiring me in all sorts of ways; JK; Patrick Friesen, for naming me, and sticking by; Carol Shields and Jan Horner, for serving on the Thesis Examining Committee for an earlier version of this manuscript; Catherine Hunter, for selecting *Holding the Dark* for The Muses', and for your comfortable and gracious presence as you worked with me on the final editing, performing expert CPR (Cameron's Poetry Resuscitation—you and George formed a tag-team I couldn't have trusted more to ensure the well-being of these poems); Marijke Friesen, for a beautiful cover photograph. And thank you Marguerite Love (my mother), Scot Cameron (my brother), Heather Reid (my sister-in-law), and Roy Cameron (my father) for courageously supporting and encouraging me to write and to share my writing (and to greet the consequences!). Finally: Leonard Cohen, please find me.

I would like readers to know that the original drafts of *Holding the Dark* contained a section of poems about the loss of David Cameron (1982-94), my cousin. Out of respect for family who requested that the poems not be included, I have chosen to omit this section. Nonetheless, I want to acknowledge the presence David still occupies (for me) between "The Daughters of Silence" and "An Open Hand."

References to Ophelia (in the second and last sections) are allusions to the woman figure in John Everett Millais' painting, "Ophelia."